AI Profit:

Harnessing Artificial Intelligence
For Online Wealth Creation

Alexandre-luc Wahlström Smith

Naive

INTRODUCTION TO AI AND ONLINE WEALTH CREATION

In today's digital age, the convergence of artificial intelligence (AI) and the internet has opened up a world of possibilities for wealth creation online. As technology continues to advance at an unprecedented pace, businesses and individuals have a unique opportunity to leverage the power of AI and harness its potential for driving online prosperity.

AI, in its simplest form, refers to the development of intelligent machines that can perform tasks that typically require human intelligence. These machines are capable of processing and analyzing vast amounts of data, learning from patterns, and making informed decisions. With its ability to learn and adapt, AI holds immense promise for disrupting traditional business models and generating wealth in the digital realm.

One of the key areas where AI can have a profound impact on wealth creation is automation. By automating repetitive and time-consuming tasks, businesses can significantly increase their productivity and efficiency. AI-powered chatbots, for example, can handle customer inquiries and provide support around the clock, freeing up human resources to focus on more strategic activities. Automation not only saves time but also reduces costs, allowing businesses to scale and grow without the need for extensive manpower.

Moreover, AI enables businesses to personalize customer experiences on a whole new level. By analyzing customer data and behavior patterns, AI algorithms can deliver highly targeted and personalized content, product recommendations, and marketing campaigns. This level of personalization not only enhances customer satisfaction but also increases conversion rates and customer loyalty. Imagine receiving recommendations for products or services that perfectly align with your preferences, based on your previous interactions and online behavior. AI can make this a reality, enabling businesses to build deeper connections with their customers and drive revenue growth.

Another area where AI can drive online wealth creation is through data analytics. The explosion of digital data presents both a challenge and an opportunity for businesses. With the vast amount of data generated online every second, businesses have a goldmine of insights waiting to be unlocked. AI algorithms can analyze this data, identify trends, patterns, and correlations, and provide businesses with actionable insights for strategic decision making. These insights can range from market trends and customer preferences to supply chain optimization and marketing effectiveness. By making data-driven decisions, businesses can stay ahead of the competition, adapt quickly to changing market conditions, and drive revenue growth.

The potential for AI in online wealth creation extends beyond businesses and includes individual entrepreneurs. With the rise of online platforms, anyone can now create and market their products or services globally. AI can help individuals automate various aspects of their online businesses, from inventory management and order fulfillment to social media marketing and customer support. By leveraging AI-powered tools and platforms, individuals can streamline their operations, reach a wider audience, and maximize their income potential.

However, it is important to note that AI is not a magic wand for instant wealth creation. Like any other technology, AI requires a strategic approach and careful implementation to yield tangible results. Businesses and individuals should invest in understanding AI's capabilities, explore the available tools and platforms, and adopt a long-term mindset towards its integration into their online strategies.

Furthermore, the future of AI in online wealth creation holds even more exciting prospects. For instance, AI can be used to analyze market trends and forecast demand, helping businesses identify new opportunities and develop innovative products or services. Additionally, AI-powered virtual assistants can assist businesses and individuals in managing tasks, scheduling activities, and even providing personalized recommendations based on their preferences and habits.

The ethical implications of AI in online wealth creation also need to be considered. As AI algorithms make decisions based on data and patterns, it is crucial to ensure fairness, transparency, and accountability in their use. Striking the right balance between data-driven decision-making and sensitive issues such as privacy is vital to maintain trust in AI systems and foster sustainable wealth creation online.

In conclusion, the fusion of AI and the internet presents an unparalleled opportunity for online wealth creation. By harnessing the power of AI, businesses and individuals can automate tasks, personalize customer experiences, optimize marketing strategies, and make data-driven decisions. As AI continues to evolve, the possibilities for online prosperity are endless. So, embrace the transformative power of AI and embark on a journey to unlock the vast potential it holds for online wealth creation.

*AI Profit: Harnessing Artificial Intelligence
For Online Wealth Creation*

———

UNDERSTANDING AI: FROM BASICS TO ADVANCED CONCEPTS

In this chapter, we will take a deeper dive into the world of AI, covering basic to advanced concepts. AI, or Artificial Intelligence, is a rapidly growing field that aims to create intelligent machines capable of performing tasks that typically require human intelligence. By understanding the basics and advancing our knowledge, we can unlock the true potential of AI and harness it for various applications in different industries.

0. Introduction:

Artificial Intelligence (AI) has emerged as a groundbreaking technology that is revolutionizing industries and transforming the way we interact with machines. In this chapter, we will embark on an exciting journey to explore the depths of AI, diving into its core concepts and examining the advancements that have shaped its development. By comprehending the foundational principles and delving into advanced concepts, we will equip ourselves with a comprehensive understanding of AI's potential and its evolving relationship with our world.

1. The History and Evolution of AI:

To truly grasp the essence of AI, we must start by exploring its historical roots. The concept of artificial intelligence has existed for centuries, with early pioneers like Ada Lovelace and Alan Turing planting the seeds of AI theory. However, it was in the mid-20th century that the field of AI took shape as a distinct research area. We will delve deeper into this period, highlighting key milestones such as the Dartmouth Conference in 1956, where the term "artificial intelligence" was coined. We will also explore the groundbreaking work of researchers like John McCarthy and Marvin Minsky, who paved the way for the development of AI as a robust discipline. By examining the historical context of AI, we can appreciate the challenges faced by early researchers and the innovative solutions they devised.

2. Domains and Subfields of AI:

AI encompasses a vast array of domains and subfields, each focusing on unique aspects of intelligence replication. Let us take a closer look at some of these domains and subfields:

a. Machine Learning: Machine learning is a subfield of AI that enables machines to learn patterns from data and make predictions or decisions without being explicitly programmed. We will delve into the fundamental principles of machine learning, including supervised, unsupervised, and reinforcement learning.

b. Natural Language Processing (NLP): Natural language processing equips machines with the ability to understand and interact with human language. We will explore the challenges and techniques involved in tasks such as speech recognition, sentiment analysis, and machine translation.

c. Computer Vision: Computer vision focuses on enabling machines to understand and interpret visual information from images or videos. We will delve into topics such as image classification, object detection, and image generation, examining the underlying algorithms and advancements in this field.

d. Robotics: Robotics combines AI with physical systems to create intelligent machines that can interact with the physical world. We will explore the intersection of AI and robotics, discussing topics like autonomous navigation, robot learning, and human-robot interaction.

e. Expert Systems: Expert systems replicate human expertise in specific domains, facilitating decision-making and problem-solving. We will delve into the architecture of expert systems, rule-based reasoning, and knowledge representation techniques.

3. Types of AI Systems:
AI systems can be classified into different categories based on their capabilities. Let us explore some of these categorizations:

a. Narrow AI: Narrow AI, also known as weak AI, focuses on specific tasks and is designed to excel in a limited domain. Examples include virtual personal assistants like Siri and Google Assistant, as well as recommendation systems used in e-commerce platforms. Narrow AI systems perform exceptionally well in their designated domains but lack the ability to generalize or transfer their knowledge to other contexts.

b. General AI: General AI represents the goal of creating machines that possess human-level intelligence across a wide range of tasks. Achieving general AI involves designing systems that can understand, learn, and adapt to novel situations, similar to how a human would. However, despite significant advancements in various AI domains, achieving general AI remains a substantial challenge.

c. Artificial Superintelligence: Artificial superintelligence refers to AI systems that surpass human intelligence in virtually every aspect. While this concept remains purely speculative, it raises intriguing discussions and ethical considerations regarding the potential consequences of such advanced AI.

d. Explainable AI: As AI systems become more complex, there is a growing need for transparency and interpretability. Explainable AI aims to enhance the understandability of AI systems, allowing users to comprehend the decision-making processes and the reasoning behind them. This field explores methods for ensuring AI decisions can be explained and validated, ensuring accountability and trust.

4. Challenges and Limitations of AI:
While AI presents numerous opportunities, it also poses challenges and limitations that must be considered. Let us explore some of these challenges:

a. Ethical Considerations: The development and deployment of AI must be guided by ethical principles. This involves addressing issues such as bias, fairness, and accountability in AI systems. We must ensure that AI does not perpetuate social, gender, or racial biases and that its impact on society is carefully monitored.

b. Privacy and Security: AI systems often rely on vast amounts of personal data, raising concerns about data privacy and security. Organizations and policymakers must balance the benefits of AI with the protection of individual privacy rights.

c. Explainability: As AI systems become more complex, their decision-making processes can seem like a black box, lacking transparency and understandability. This lack of explainability raises concerns and challenges in trusting and validating AI-generated outcomes.

d. Unemployment and Workforce Transformation: The integration of AI technologies in various industries has implications for the workforce. While AI can automate routine tasks and enable efficiency, it may also disrupt certain job markets and require a shift in the skills demanded in the workforce. Addressing these challenges involves proactive measures such as reskilling and upskilling the workforce.

5. Real-world Applications and Case Studies:

Throughout the chapter, we will provide real-world examples and case studies to illustrate how AI is being applied in various industries. Let us explore a few of these applications:

a. Healthcare: AI is revolutionizing healthcare by enabling more accurate diagnoses,
personalized treatment plans, and drug discovery. We will explore examples such as AI powered medical imaging, predictive analytics, and virtual healthcare assistants.

b. Finance: AI is transforming the finance industry by automating manual tasks, detecting fraud, and providing personalized financial recommendations. We will delve into areas such as algorithmic trading, credit scoring models, and chatbots for customer support.

c. Manufacturing: AI is optimizing manufacturing processes by enabling predictive maintenance, quality control, and supply chain optimization. We will explore how AI is used in areas like robotics in manufacturing, demand forecasting, and anomaly detection.

d. Transportation: AI is reshaping the transportation sector by paving the way for autonomous vehicles, optimizing traffic management, and enhancing logistics. We will examine the role of AI in self-driving cars, predictive maintenance of vehicles, and route optimization.

These examples, among many others, showcase the tangible impact of AI in various industries, highlighting its potential to drive innovation and improve efficiency.

By the conclusion of this chapter, you will possess a comprehensive understanding of AI, ranging from its historical origins to advanced concepts. This knowledge will not only serve as a strong foundation for the subsequent chapters but will also empower you to navigate the ever-evolving landscape of AI and unlock its transformative potential. So, let us embark on this journey of discovery and immerse ourselves in the captivating world of AI.

6. Machine Learning Algorithms and Techniques:
Machine learning lies at the heart of AI, enabling machines to learn from data and improve their performance over time. Understanding the various machine learning algorithms and techniques is crucial for developing effective AI systems. In this section, we will explore different types of machine learning algorithms:

a. Supervised Learning: Supervised learning involves training a model to learn a mapping between input data and corresponding output labels. We will delve into algorithms such as linear regression, logistic regression, support vector machines (SVM), and decision trees.

b. Unsupervised Learning: Unsupervised learning aims to find patterns and relationships in data without any provided labels. Clustering algorithms, such as K-means and hierarchical clustering, as well as dimensionality reduction techniques like principal component analysis (PCA), will be discussed in detail.

c. Reinforcement Learning: Reinforcement learning involves training an agent to interact with an environment and learn optimal actions through a reward signal. We will explore concepts such as Markov Decision Processes (MDPs), Q-learning, and policy gradients.

d. Deep Learning: Deep learning utilizes neural networks with multiple layers to learn complex representations from data. Convolutional neural networks (CNNs) excel in image recognition tasks, recurrent neural networks (RNNs) are used for sequence data, and generative adversarial networks (GANs) enable data generation. We will delve into the architectures, training methods, and applications of deep learning models.

7. AI Ethics and Responsible AI:

As AI continues to become more pervasive, it is crucial to consider the ethical implications and ensure responsible AI development. The field of AI ethics focuses on addressing ethical concerns, biases, and social implications. We will explore key ethical considerations, such as fairness, transparency, and accountability in AI systems. Additionally, we will discuss guidelines and frameworks for responsible AI development, including privacy protection, data governance, and algorithmic transparency.

8. AI in the Future:

The future of AI is boundless, with new advancements continually emerging. In this section, we will delve into emerging trends and possibilities shaping the future of AI:

a. Explainable AI: Explainable AI will become increasingly important as AI systems become more complex. Efforts to provide interpretable explanations for AI decisions will continue to advance.

b. Edge Computing: With the growth of Internet of Things (IoT) devices, AI will be more decentralized and integrated into these devices. Edge computing will enable AI processing to happen locally on the devices themselves, reducing latency and enhancing privacy.

c. Autonomous Systems: Autonomous systems, such as self-driving cars and drones, will continue to evolve, with advancements in perception, decision-making, and planning.

d. AI and Healthcare: AI will play a significant role in healthcare, from aiding diagnosis to personalized medicine. The integration of AI with electronic health records, wearables, and remote monitoring will enhance patient care and revolutionize healthcare delivery.

e. AI and Sustainability: AI can contribute to sustainability efforts by optimizing energy consumption, reducing waste, and improving resource management. From smart grids to precision agriculture, AI can drive sustainable practices in various industries.
Embracing the potential of AI while addressing its challenges and ethical aspects will shape the future trajectory of this technology. By keeping a pulse on the latest advancements and trends, we can actively contribute to the responsible development and application of AI.

In conclusion, AI is a vast and dynamic field that encompasses various domains, algorithms, and applications. By understanding its historical evolution, exploring its subfields, and delving into advanced concepts, we can gain a holistic understanding of AI's potential and its impact on society. Furthermore, by considering ethical aspects and promoting responsible AI development, we can ensure that AI technology benefits humanity in a positive and sustainable manner. Armed with this knowledge, we can navigate the rapidly evolving AI landscape and actively contribute to its growth and advancement.

AI Profit: Harnessing Artificial Intelligence
For Online Wealth Creation

———————

THE INTERSECTION OF AI AND ONLINE BUSINESS

In today's rapidly evolving digital landscape, artificial intelligence (AI) has emerged as a transformative force, revolutionizing the way businesses operate online. The seamless integration of AI technologies with online business has led to improved efficiency, enhanced customer experiences, and increased profitability. In this chapter, we will delve deeper into the various ways in which AI intersects with online business and explore the profound impact it has had on diverse industries.

0. Introduction: The Rise of AI in Online Business

Artificial intelligence (AI) technology encompasses a wide range of techniques that allow machines to mimic human intelligence and perform tasks that traditionally required human effort. The convergence of AI and online business has paved the way for groundbreaking innovations and has fundamentally transformed the digital landscape. From personalized customer experiences to predictive analytics, automation to voice technology, AI has enabled businesses to gain a competitive edge and thrive in the ever-evolving online marketplace.

1. Personalization: Enhancing Customer Experiences

AI algorithms have become invaluable in providing

personalized experiences to online customers. Through advanced machine learning techniques, businesses can analyze vast amounts of user data, such as browsing behavior, purchase history, and social media interactions, to create targeted and relevant recommendations. By understanding individual preferences and needs, AI-powered recommendation systems enable businesses to increase customer engagement, boost conversions, and foster loyalty.

In addition to personalized recommendations, AI-driven customer service chatbots have transformed the way businesses interact with online customers. These conversational agents leverage natural language processing (NLP) algorithms to comprehend and respond to customer queries promptly and accurately. Chatbots not only provide instant support but can also assist in making purchase decisions, resolving issues, and offering
proactive assistance. By merging the efficiency of automation with the empathy of human-like interactions, businesses can deliver superior customer experiences.

2. Predictive Analytics: Anticipating Market Trends and Opportunities

The integration of AI in online business has unlocked the power of predictive analytics. By leveraging machine learning algorithms, businesses can analyze vast amounts of data and extract meaningful insights. AI algorithms can identify patterns, trends, and correlations, empowering businesses to make accurate predictions about customer behavior, market trends, and demand forecasting. Armed with these insights, businesses can make informed decisions, optimize marketing strategies, and identify new business opportunities.

Moreover, AI-based predictive analytics can enhance inventory management and supply chain optimization. By analyzing historical data, businesses can accurately estimate future demand, reduce wastage, and optimize stock levels, ensuring smooth operations and improved profitability.

3. Automation: Accelerating Efficiency and Enhancing Processes

AI technologies enable businesses to automate mundane and repetitive tasks, freeing up valuable time and resources. For example, computer vision algorithms can automate image recognition and tagging, streamlining product catalog creation and enhancing search functionality on e-commerce platforms. This automation minimizes human errors, reduces manual effort, and significantly enhances operational efficiency.

Moreover, AI-based automation extends to various aspects of online business, such as customer support, content generation, and fraud detection. Chatbots, powered by AI, can handle a vast array of customer queries, providing 24/7 support at scale. AI algorithms are also capable of generating personalized content, facilitating automated email marketing campaigns, and curating engaging social media posts. Additionally, AI-powered fraud detection systems can detect and respond to potential fraudulent activities in real-time, safeguarding businesses and customers alike.

4. Voice Technology: Revolutionizing Customer Interaction

Voice assistants, powered by AI, have revolutionized the online business landscape by enabling voice-based transactions, improved customer service, and seamless interactions. Virtual assistants like Amazon's Alexa, Apple's Siri, or Google Assistant provide users with instant access to information, product recommendations, and even enable voice-based purchases. With the growing popularity of smart speakers, voice technology has become an essential channel for businesses to engage with customers, providing a frictionless and convenient shopping experience.

Furthermore, AI-powered voice recognition and sentiment analysis allow businesses to gain valuable insights into customer experiences, preferences, and pain points. By understanding customer sentiment, businesses can adapt their strategies, improve product offerings, and personalize interactions further.

5. Ethical Considerations: Navigating Responsibility and Fairness

While AI offers tremendous opportunities for online businesses, it also raises ethical considerations. Businesses need to prioritize transparency, fairness, and accountability in their use of AI technologies. Ensuring the protection of customer privacy, avoiding algorithmic bias, and maintaining data security are crucial challenges that must be addressed. By adhering to ethical guidelines and adopting responsible AI practices, businesses can build trust with customers and maintain long-term success in the ever evolving online business landscape.

6. Emerging Trends: Reinventing Online Business

As AI continues to advance, new trends are emerging that further redefine the intersection of AI and online business. One such trend is the rise of virtual reality (VR) and augmented reality (AR) technologies. AI algorithms combined with VR and AR components offer immersive product experiences, enabling customers to visualize products in real-world scenarios before making a purchase. This trend transforms the online shopping experience by bridging the gap between physical and digital realms.

Additionally, AI-powered chatbots are evolving into

more intelligent and contextually aware conversational assistants. Natural language understanding and generation capabilities are improving, allowing chatbots to engage in more sophisticated conversations and provide even more comprehensive support. Incorporating emotions and empathy into AI-driven interactions may become a prominent direction, enhancing the overall customer experience.

In conclusion, the intersection of AI and online business has brought about unprecedented advancements in efficiency, customer experience, and profitability. From personalization to predictive analytics, automation to voice technology, AI continues to transform the digital landscape, offering businesses immense opportunities for growth and success. Leveraging AI technologies enables businesses to gain a competitive edge, adapt to changing customer expectations, and thrive in the fast-paced world of online business. By embracing AI with ethical considerations, adopting emerging trends, and fostering responsible AI practices,
businesses can navigate the evolving digital landscape and shape a brighter future for the online business ecosystem.

*AI Profit: Harnessing Artificial Intelligence
For Online Wealth Creation*

———

AI TOOLS AND THEIR APPLICATIONS

Artificial Intelligence (AI) has revolutionized the online business landscape, providing businesses with a wide array of tools to optimize operations, enhance customer experiences, and drive growth. In this chapter, we will delve deeper into various AI tools and their detailed applications in the realm of online business, providing a comprehensive understanding of their capabilities and potential.

1. Natural Language Processing (NLP):
NLP is a critical AI tool that empowers computers to understand and analyze human language. Its applications in online business are vast and multifaceted. Chatbots and virtual assistants powered by NLP can accurately interpret and respond to customer inquiries, streamlining customer service operations and ensuring prompt and accurate support. By understanding user intent, sentiment, and context, NLP enhances engagement and customer satisfaction, ultimately bringing tangible business benefits.

Furthermore, NLP is extensively used in sentiment analysis. By automatically analyzing customer feedback, social media posts, and reviews, businesses can gain valuable insights into customer sentiment, allowing them to quickly address concerns, improve products or services, and enhance brand reputation. NLP also plays a crucial role in content generation, enabling businesses to automate the creation of personalized emails, product descriptions, or customer communications, saving time and resources.

2. Recommendation Systems:

Recommendation systems leverage machine learning algorithms to provide personalized suggestions to users. Their applications in online business are diverse and impactful. E-commerce platforms utilize recommendation systems to showcase products that align with a user's preferences, browsing history, and purchase history. This personalized approach enhances the user experience, increases engagement, and ultimately drives sales.

Streaming services also heavily rely on recommendation systems. By analyzing user activities, content preferences, and viewer patterns, these platforms can provide tailored recommendations that keep users engaged and subscribed. Social media networks utilize recommendation systems to curate customized content feeds for users, promoting relevant posts and advertisements based on their interests, connections, and online behavior.

3. Data Analytics:

AI-powered data analytics tools empower businesses to analyze vast amounts of data in real-time, extracting valuable insights. These tools utilize machine learning algorithms to identify patterns, trends, and correlations, providing businesses with actionable intelligence. The applications of data analytics in online business are varied and crucial for success.

By analyzing customer data, businesses can gain a deep understanding of their target audience, including demographics, preferences, and behaviors. This knowledge enables businesses to create personalized marketing campaigns, optimize website design and user experience, and personalize product offerings. Data analytics also allows for predictive analytics, empowering businesses to anticipate customer needs and behaviors, optimize inventory management, and streamline supply chain operations.

Furthermore, data analytics find applications in conversion rate optimization (CRO). By studying website metrics, user behavior, and A/B testing results, businesses gain insights into factors that impact conversion rates, allowing them to make data-driven decisions to improve user experience, optimize sales funnels, and increase conversions.

4. Image and Video Recognition:

Image and video recognition tools have become indispensable for online businesses, particularly in the e-commerce industry. These AI-powered tools enable businesses to automatically analyze and categorize visual content, facilitating faster product tagging, automated inventory management, and improved search capabilities. The applications of image and video recognition in online business are diverse.

E-commerce platforms benefit from image recognition by automatically identifying products within images and linking them to the appropriate listings. This eliminates the need for lengthy manual tagging processes, improves the accuracy of search results, and enhances the overall shopping experience. Image recognition also assists businesses in monitoring their brand presence online, identifying instances of unauthorized product listings or brand misuse.

Video recognition tools enable businesses to analyze and categorize video content, facilitating targeted advertisement placement and content recommendation on video sharing platforms. By understanding the context, objects, and actions within videos, businesses can target specific audiences, optimize ad spend, and enhance engagement.

5. Fraud Detection and Prevention:

AI is extensively applied in fraud detection and prevention in online business. Machine learning algorithms analyze large volumes of transaction data, identifying patterns and anomalies that indicate fraudulent activities. By quickly flagging suspicious transactions, businesses can mitigate risks, protect their customers' financial security, and safeguard their own reputation.

Fraud detection AI tools utilize machine learning algorithms to create models that continuously learn from new data. These models can adapt to new fraud patterns, identify emerging threats, and stay ahead of evolving techniques used by fraudsters. The applications of AI in fraud detection span across various industries, including banking, e-commerce, insurance, and online payment platforms.

In conclusion, understanding and harnessing the power of AI tools in online business is crucial for success in the digital age. The detailed insights provided in this chapter highlight the diverse range of AI tools available and their applications across different aspects of online business. By leveraging AI effectively, businesses can optimize processes, drive growth, and provide exceptional customer experiences, ultimately gaining a competitive advantage in the dynamic online business landscape.

AI Profit: Harnessing Artificial Intelligence
For Online Wealth Creation

CASE STUDIES: SUCCESSFUL AI-DRIVEN ONLINE BUSINESSES

In today's rapidly evolving business landscape, online ventures are capitalizing on the transformative power of Artificial Intelligence (AI) to drive their growth and success. In this chapter, we will delve into real-life case studies of successful online businesses that have leveraged AI to revolutionize their operations and enhance customer experiences. Through these examples, readers will gain a deeper understanding of the practical applications and benefits of incorporating AI into their own online ventures.

Case Study 1: Company A - Revolutionizing Customer Service with AI

Company A is an e-commerce platform that sought to revolutionize the customer service experience by implementing AI-powered chatbots. These intelligent chatbots were designed to analyze customer queries and previous interactions, enabling them to provide instant and personalized support. By utilizing natural language processing and machine learning algorithms, these chatbots could understand customer intents, answer complex queries, and even resolve issues autonomously. Thanks to this advanced AI-driven customer service approach, Company A witnessed a significant reduction in response times, increased customer satisfaction rates, and improved operational efficiency. The ability to provide round-the-clock support without human intervention not only saved costs but also led to increased customer loyalty and retention.

Case Study 2: Company B - Enhancing Product Recommendations with AI Company B, an online retail store, recognized the importance of personalized product recommendations in driving customer engagement and boosting sales. To achieve this, they implemented AI algorithms to enhance their recommendation system. By analyzing vast amounts of customer behavior, preferences, and purchase history data, the AI-powered recommendation engine was able to generate highly accurate and relevant product recommendations. Leveraging techniques such as collaborative filtering, natural language processing, and deep learning, the system went beyond generic product suggestions. Instead, it provided personalized recommendations that aligned with each customer's unique tastes and preferences. As a result, Company B experienced increased conversion rates, higher average order values, and an overall improved user experience. By leveraging AI to better understand their customers' needs, Company B was able to stay ahead of competitors and nurture long-lasting customer relationships.

Case Study 3: Company C - Optimizing Online Advertising Campaigns with AI Company C, a digital marketing agency, understood the significance of optimizing online advertising campaigns to achieve maximum results for their clients. To achieve this, they employed AI technology to revolutionize their advertising strategy. By harnessing the power of machine learning algorithms, the AI system continuously monitored and analyzed the performance of various ad campaigns in real-time. It utilized data on customer demographics, browsing behavior, and conversion rates to dynamically adjust bidding strategies, ad targeting, and creative elements. With this AI-driven approach, Company C achieved a level of precision and effectiveness that far surpassed traditional manual optimization methods. As a result, their clients experienced an incredible improvement in their return on investment (ROI) for their advertising campaigns. By leveraging AI to optimize their advertising efforts, Company C became a trusted partner for businesses seeking to make the most of their online ad spend.

Case Study 4: Company D - Streamlining Supply Chain Management with AI Company D, an online marketplace, faced numerous complexities in managing their supply chain efficiently. To overcome these challenges, they turned to AI technologies to streamline their supply chain management processes. By analyzing historical data, market trends, weather patterns, and other external factors, the AI system accurately predicted product demand and optimized inventory management. This allowed Company D to maintain optimal stock levels, reduce stockouts, minimize overstocking, and ultimately improve operational efficiency. The AI system's ability to forecast demand not only saved costs but also ensured better customer satisfaction by reducing delivery delays and backorders. Company D's AI-driven supply chain management approach positioned them as a leader in their industry, ensuring smooth operations and gaining a competitive edge over their peers.

These case studies serve as compelling examples of how AI can revolutionize online businesses across various industries. They demonstrate the diverse applications of AI, ranging from customer service and product recommendations to advertising campaigns and supply chain management. By studying these successful AI-driven online businesses, readers gain valuable insights into the transformative potential of AI for their own ventures.

In the subsequent chapters, we will explore the methodologies, tools, and approaches employed by these businesses in greater detail. Readers will gain a comprehensive understanding of how to leverage AI for online wealth creation and long-term success.

*AI Profit: Harnessing Artificial Intelligence
For Online Wealth Creation*

———

MACHINE LEARNING AND ITS ROLE IN ONLINE BUSINESS

Introduction

With the exponential growth of digital technologies and online platforms, businesses are constantly searching for innovative ways to gain a competitive edge. Machine learning, a branch of artificial intelligence, has emerged as a powerful tool that can transform the landscape of online business. In this chapter, we will delve into the details of machine learning and explore its significant role in enhancing various aspects of online business.

1. Improving Customer Experiences

Machine learning algorithms have the ability to analyze vast amounts of customer data, enabling businesses to gain valuable insights into customer behaviors, preferences, and needs. By leveraging this data, online businesses can offer personalized experiences to their customers. For example, e-commerce platforms can use machine learning algorithms to make tailored product recommendations based on browsing and purchasing histories. This personalization not only increases customer satisfaction but also boosts conversion rates.

Moreover, machine learning algorithms can be employed to optimize user interfaces and website layouts. By analyzing how customers interact with a website, businesses can identify potential pain points, optimize navigation, and enhance the overall user experience. This results in increased customer engagement and prolonged website visits.

2. Fraud Detection and Prevention

The evolving nature of online transactions poses significant challenges in terms of fraud detection and prevention. Traditional rule-based systems often fail to keep pace with the sophistication of modern fraud techniques. Machine learning, however, offers a more effective solution. By analyzing multiple variables such as user behavior, transaction history, and device information, machine learning algorithms can detect patterns indicative of fraudulent activities. This enables businesses to integrate real-time fraud detection systems, protect themselves from financial losses, and maintain the trust of their customers.

Furthermore, machine learning algorithms can adapt to new fraud patterns and identify emerging threats. They continuously learn from new data, enabling businesses to stay one step ahead of fraudsters. This dynamic approach to fraud detection ensures that online businesses are equipped with the necessary tools to combat evolving fraud strategies.

3. Optimizing Marketing Strategies

Machine learning algorithms can analyze customer data to identify patterns, segment customers, and predict their behavior. This information can greatly enhance marketing strategies for online businesses. By understanding customer preferences and purchasing patterns, businesses can create targeted advertisements that are more likely to resonate with their audience. Machine learning algorithms can also help optimize marketing budgets by identifying the most effective channels and campaigns, leading to higher return on investment.

Moreover, machine learning algorithms can analyze the

success of previous marketing campaigns and provide insights to optimize future campaigns. They can identify which factors, such as demographics, timing, or promotional offers, contribute to campaign success. This information allows businesses to fine-tune their marketing strategies, allocate resources more efficiently, and improve overall campaign performance.

4. Predicting Customer Churn

Customer retention is vital for the success of any online business. Machine learning algorithms can analyze historical customer data to identify patterns that predict customer churn. By proactively identifying customers at risk of leaving, businesses can take necessary measures to engage with them and prevent churn. This could include personalized offers, improved customer support, or a tailored loyalty program. Predicting customer churn allows businesses to maximize customer lifetime value, reduce acquisition costs, and ultimately improve profitability.

Furthermore, machine learning algorithms can provide insights into the root causes of churn. They can identify the factors that commonly lead to customer attrition, such as pricing, product issues, or poor customer service. By addressing these underlying issues, businesses can reduce churn rates and foster stronger relationships with their customers.

5. Dynamic Pricing

Setting the right price for products and services is a critical factor in maximizing revenue and staying competitive. Machine learning algorithms can analyze market trends, competitor pricing, and customer data to determine optimal price points. By constantly analyzing and adjusting prices based on supply, demand, and customer behavior, businesses can implement dynamic pricing strategies. This approach ensures that prices remain competitive while maximizing profitability. Additionally, machine learning algorithms can assist in predicting demand fluctuations and recommending discounts or promotions to stimulate sales during low-demand periods.

Furthermore, machine learning algorithms can analyze and optimize pricing strategies based on competitor behavior. By monitoring competitor pricing in real-time, businesses can respond quickly and effectively, ensuring they remain competitive in the market. This dynamic pricing capability, combined with insights from customer behavior, allows businesses to maximize revenue while maintaining a competitive edge.

6. Supply Chain Optimization

Online businesses rely heavily on streamlined supply chain operations for timely deliveries and efficient inventory management. Machine learning algorithms can leverage predictive analytics to forecast demand patterns, optimize inventory levels, and improve logistic operations. By considering various factors, such as historical sales data, market trends, and lead times, machine learning algorithms assist in making accurate demand forecasts. This allows businesses to optimize their inventory levels, minimize stockouts, and reduce wastage. In turn, this improves the efficiency of supply chain operations and ensures a seamless customer experience.

Furthermore, machine learning algorithms can identify inefficiencies and bottlenecks in the supply chain. They can analyze data from various sources, such as suppliers, warehouses, and transportation, to identify areas of improvement. This could involve optimizing delivery routes, reducing lead times, or improving supplier relationships. By optimizing supply chain operations, businesses can reduce costs, improve customer satisfaction, and gain a competitive advantage in the market.

Conclusion

Machine learning has revolutionized the way online businesses operate by leveraging large datasets, advanced algorithms, and computing power. From improving customer experiences through personalization, detecting and preventing fraud, optimizing marketing strategies, predicting customer churn, implementing dynamic pricing, and streamlining supply chain operations, machine learning has a profound impact on various facets of online business. By harnessing the power of machine learning, businesses can unlock new opportunities, gain a competitive advantage, and build long-lasting relationships with their customers in the fast-paced digital landscape.

AI Profit: Harnessing Artificial Intelligence
For Online Wealth Creation

———

AI AND E-COMMERCE: A PERFECT MATCH

E-commerce has revolutionized the way we buy and sell products and services, and the integration of AI technology has taken this revolution to new heights. In this chapter, we will explore the perfect match between AI and e-commerce, delving deeper into the synergies that exist between these two domains.

AI, or artificial intelligence, has transformed the e-commerce landscape by providing businesses with a wide range of tools and capabilities to enhance customer experiences, streamline operations, and ultimately drive revenue growth. One of the key areas where AI has made a significant impact is in personalized recommendations.

Through the analysis of vast amounts of customer data, AI algorithms can generate highly accurate and tailored product recommendations for individual users. By understanding each customer's preferences, browsing history, and purchase behavior, AI can suggest relevant products or services, leading to increased customer satisfaction and sales.

AI-powered recommendation systems rely on various techniques such as collaborative filtering, content-based filtering, and hybrid approaches. Collaborative filtering analyzes user behavior and preferences to identify patterns and similarities with other users. It then recommends items that similar users have enjoyed. Content-based filtering, on the other hand, focuses on the characteristics and attributes of items to make recommendations. Hybrid approaches combine both collaborative and content-based techniques to provide the most accurate and diverse suggestions.

Furthermore, AI-powered chatbots have become an indispensable tool for e-commerce businesses, providing instantaneous support and engagement with customers. These chatbots can efficiently answer questions, provide product information, and even assist with the purchase process, eliminating the need for human intervention in many cases. Natural Language Processing (NLP) techniques enable chatbots to understand and respond to customer queries effectively, creating a seamless and personalized conversational experience.

Moreover, AI can be leveraged to optimize supply chain management in e-commerce. With the ability to analyze and predict demand patterns, AI algorithms can help businesses in inventory management, order fulfillment, and logistics. By efficiently managing stock levels and streamlining delivery processes, e-commerce companies can minimize costs and provide faster and more reliable service to their customers.

Demand forecasting is a critical component of supply chain management in e-commerce. AI algorithms utilize historical sales data, market trends, and external factors like seasonality or promotions to predict future demand accurately. These forecasts can help businesses plan their inventory levels, anticipate replenishment needs, and avoid stockouts or overstocks. By doing so, AI enables a more efficient supply chain, reducing carrying costs and improving profitability.

Fraud detection and prevention have also seen immense improvements with the incorporation of AI in e-commerce platforms. Machine learning algorithms can analyze vast amounts of transaction data to identify patterns and anomalies associated with fraudulent activities. By flagging suspicious transactions in real-time, AI can help businesses prevent financial losses and maintain the trust of their customers.

AI-based fraud detection systems employ advanced techniques such as anomaly detection, pattern recognition, and behavioral analysis. These systems establish baseline patterns of normal user behavior and can identify any deviations from these patterns, raising alerts for potential fraudulent transactions. The continuous learning capabilities of AI algorithms allow them to adapt and evolve alongside emerging fraud patterns, providing ongoing protection against evolving threats.

In addition to these benefits, AI has also opened doors for new business models in e-commerce, such as virtual marketplaces and personalized pricing. AI algorithms can analyze market trends, competitor data, and customer insights to support decision-making and enable businesses to offer unique and tailored shopping experiences.

Virtual marketplaces, enabled by AI, connect buyers and sellers on a digital platform, providing a wide range of products and services without the need for physical stores or inventory. These marketplaces utilize AI algorithms to match buyers' preferences with sellers' offerings, creating a personalized experience that enhances customer satisfaction and drives engagement.

Personalized pricing is another area where AI and e-commerce intersect. By analyzing customer data, AI algorithms can determine an individual's willingness to pay and dynamically adjust prices accordingly. This dynamic pricing strategy accounts for factors like the customer's browsing behavior, purchase history, and market conditions to offer personalized discounts or promotions. This approach not only maximizes revenue for businesses but also provides tailored and fair pricing for consumers.

However, it is important to acknowledge that while AI brings significant advantages to e-commerce, it also raises concerns regarding data privacy, algorithm bias, and job displacement. These ethical considerations must be addressed to ensure that AI is harnessed responsibly and for the benefit of all stakeholders involved.

To mitigate privacy concerns, businesses must prioritize transparency and obtain clear consent when collecting and using customer data. Data encryption and robust security measures should also be implemented to protect sensitive information from unauthorized access.

Furthermore, addressing algorithm bias is essential to ensure fair treatment for all customers. AI algorithms can inadvertently perpetuate biases present in the data they are trained on. Businesses need to regularly audit and update their algorithms to minimize bias and ensure that recommendations, pricing, and other AI-driven decisions remain fair and equitable.

Regarding job displacement, it is important to recognize that while AI may automate certain tasks, it also creates new opportunities. As repetitive and mundane tasks are automated, employees can focus on more creative and strategic roles. Businesses should invest in reskilling and upskilling programs for their workforce, enabling them to adapt to the changing demands of the AI-powered e-commerce landscape.

In summary, the synergy between AI and e-commerce is

reshaping the way we shop, and businesses that embrace this partnership are well-positioned to thrive in the digital era. With personalized recommendations, AI-powered chatbots, optimized supply chain management, fraud detection, and new business models, AI is revolutionizing every aspect of e-commerce, setting the stage for a future where convenience, personalization, and efficiency are at the forefront of the shopping experience. By addressing ethical concerns and leveraging AI responsibly, society can fully benefit from the immense potential that AI brings to the world of e-commerce.

AI Profit: Harnessing Artificial Intelligence
For Online Wealth Creation

———————

USING AI TOOLS FOR MARKET ANALYSIS

Market analysis is a critical process that provides businesses with detailed insights into consumer behavior, identifies trends, and helps make informed business decisions. Over the years, the advent of AI technology has revolutionized market analysis, empowering businesses with deeper understanding and more accurate predictions.

One of the key advantages of using AI tools for market analysis is their exceptional ability to process vast amounts of data in real-time. Compared to traditional market analysis methods that often rely on manual data collection and analysis, AI tools can quickly analyze large datasets, extracting valuable insights and identifying patterns that might have otherwise been missed by human analysts.

AI tools incorporate various techniques such as machine learning, natural language processing, and statistical modeling. These techniques enable AI algorithms to detect hidden patterns, correlations, and anomalies, providing businesses with a comprehensive understanding of their target market. By analyzing diverse data sources such as social media, consumer reviews, sales data, and market trends, AI tools can uncover valuable insights and facilitate data-driven decision-making.

Predictive analytics is another significant advantage offered by AI tools in market analysis. By analyzing historical data and applying machine learning algorithms, AI can predict future patterns and help businesses make informed decisions about pricing, product development, and marketing strategies. For instance, AI algorithms can analyze consumer preferences, purchase history, and demographic data to predict which products will be the most successful in the market. This predictive power allows businesses to allocate resources effectively, minimize risks, and maximize opportunities.

Automation is a key attribute of AI tools that significantly enhances market analysis. These tools automate repetitive tasks such as data collection, data cleansing, and data preprocessing, saving valuable time for analysts. Compared to traditional methods where analysts spend a substantial amount of time gathering and cleaning data, automation allows them to focus on more strategic tasks, like data interpretation and strategy development. Through automation, AI tools can efficiently handle large datasets, thereby improving the depth and scope of the analysis.

Moreover, using AI tools for market analysis minimizes the risk of human error and bias, ensuring reliable and accurate results. AI algorithms can perform complex calculations and statistical analyses with precision, eliminating the influence of human subjectivity. As a result, businesses can rely on the accuracy of the insights gained from AI tools, enabling them to make more confident decisions based on objective data.

AI tools also excel in market segmentation, a critical aspect of understanding target markets. By analyzing customer data and behavior patterns, AI algorithms can segment markets more effectively, allowing businesses to tailor their marketing efforts to specific customer segments. Traditional market segmentation methods often rely on assumptions or limited information about customer preferences. However, AI tools enable businesses to analyze vast amounts of data, uncovering deeper insights into consumer behavior and preferences. This level of personalization can significantly improve the effectiveness of marketing campaigns, leading to higher conversion rates and increased customer satisfaction.

Additionally, AI tools prove invaluable in monitoring and analyzing competitor activity. By analyzing competitor data and social media trends, AI algorithms provide insights into market gaps, potential threats, and opportunities for growth. This competitive intelligence gives businesses a significant advantage in the ever-evolving market landscape. For example, AI tools can monitor competitor pricing strategies, promotional campaigns, or product launches, providing businesses with valuable insights to make reactive decisions and stay ahead of the competition.

However, it is crucial to emphasize that using AI tools for market analysis does not replace the need for human expertise and judgment. While AI can provide valuable insights and automate certain tasks, human analysts play a critical role in interpreting the results, making strategic decisions, and understanding the broader market context. Human analysts provide the necessary context, creativity, and critical thinking required to derive actionable insights from the data provided by AI tools.

In conclusion, AI tools have transformed market analysis by providing detailed insights, predictive analytics, automation, and enhanced market segmentation capabilities. By leveraging AI technology, businesses can gain a competitive edge, make data-driven decisions, and maximize their potential for success in the market. The constant advancements in AI open up new possibilities in market analysis, empowering businesses to make smarter, more informed choices that drive growth and profitability. Combining the power of AI tools with human expertise allows businesses to unlock new opportunities in the market and stay ahead of the competition.

*AI Profit: Harnessing Artificial Intelligence
For Online Wealth Creation*

CASE STUDIES: AI IN MARKET ANALYSIS

As markets become increasingly competitive and complex, businesses are turning to AI to gain a competitive advantage, make informed decisions, and drive growth and profitability. In this chapter, we will explore a series of case studies that highlight the extensive application and effectiveness of AI in market analysis. These in-depth case studies offer valuable insights into how AI can revolutionize market analysis, paving the way for data driven strategies and successful business outcomes.

Case Study 1: XYZ Retail Company
XYZ Retail Company, a multinational corporation with a diverse product line and a large customer base, recognized the need to improve their market analysis capabilities. They aimed to identify customer preferences, predict market trends, optimize pricing strategies, and personalize their marketing efforts. By implementing AI technologies, XYZ Retail Company was able to analyze vast amounts of data, including customer purchase history, browsing behavior, and social media interactions. Advanced machine learning algorithms aided in segmenting the customer base, identifying patterns and trends, and understanding the specific demands of different customer segments. Armed with this valuable insight, they tailored their marketing efforts accordingly, resulting in a significant increase in

customer satisfaction, sales revenue, and market share. The implementation of AI not only allowed XYZ Retail Company to stay ahead of the competition but also enabled them to deliver personalized experiences that resonated with their customers.

Case Study 2: ABC Tech Startup

ABC Tech Startup, an innovative startup operating in the technology industry, recognized the importance of market analysis in determining the potential demand for their new product. They wanted to make data-driven decisions regarding product features, pricing strategies, and target audience. By leveraging AI algorithms, ABC Tech Startup collected and analyzed comprehensive market data, including competitor analysis, customer reviews, and online surveys. AI-powered sentiment analysis tools allowed them to gauge customer sentiment and identify key pain points in existing products. With this valuable insight, they refined their product offerings, aligning them with customer needs and preferences. The result was a successful product launch, market disruption, and rapid growth. The use of AI not only helped ABC Tech Startup make informed decisions but also enabled them to address customer pain points effectively, forging strong customer relationships.

Case Study 3: DEF Financial Services Firm

DEF Financial Services Firm aimed to enhance their investment strategies and improve portfolio management for their clients. They recognized the potential of AI-powered predictive analytics in analyzing historical financial data, market trends, and macroeconomic factors. By utilizing machine learning algorithms, DEF Financial Services Firm identified patterns in stock price movements, predicted market shifts, and optimized portfolio allocations. This data-driven approach led to improved investment performance, reduced risks, and higher returns for their clients, establishing the firm as a trusted and successful player in the financial services industry. The incorporation of AI empowered DEF Financial Services Firm to make more informed investment decisions, offering their clients a competitive edge in the market.

Case Study 4: GHI Market Research Agency

GHI Market Research Agency aimed to deliver more accurate and insightful market research reports to their clients. They recognized the limitations of traditional research methods and saw the potential of AI in enhancing their capabilities. By harnessing AI technologies, GHI Market Research Agency automated the data collection process, eliminating human error and bias. Machine learning algorithms were utilized to analyze vast datasets, identify correlations, and generate actionable insights. The integration of natural language processing allowed them to perform sentiment analysis on social media and online reviews, providing real-time analysis of customer opinions and feedback. This innovative and data-driven approach revolutionized their research capabilities, enabling them to deliver more robust and reliable market research reports. The AI-powered insights enabled GHI Market Research Agency's clients to make data-driven decisions, optimize their market strategies, and achieve better business outcomes.

These comprehensive case studies demonstrate the transformative power of AI in market analysis. By harnessing AI technologies, businesses across various industries can gain valuable insights, make data-driven decisions, and drive growth and profitability. Whether it involves improving customer segmentation, predicting market trends, refining product offerings, or optimizing investment strategies, AI proves to be a game-changer in market analysis. Embracing AI allows companies to stay ahead of the competition, adapt to changing market dynamics, and unlock new opportunities for success. As technology continues to evolve, we can expect even more advanced AI applications in market analysis, further revolutionizing the way businesses understand and respond to their markets.

AI Profit: Harnessing Artificial Intelligence
For Online Wealth Creation

———

CLOUD COMPUTING AND AI: A POWERFUL COMBINATION

Introduction:
Cloud computing and artificial intelligence (AI) have become two intertwined technologies that are reshaping the business landscape. Together, they offer immense potential for organizations to scale, optimize processes, and leverage data-driven insights. In this chapter, we explore the profound impact and benefits of combining cloud computing and AI, as well as the challenges and considerations that accompany this partnership.

1. Harnessing the Power of Cloud Computing:
Cloud computing provides businesses with access to computing resources and services, including storage, processing power, and software applications, delivered over the internet. This eliminates the need for significant investments in on-premises infrastructure and offers unparalleled flexibility and scalability. By utilizing the cloud, organizations can achieve dynamic allocation of resources based on demand, resulting in cost savings and improved operational efficiency. The cloud acts as an ideal platform for AI deployment, enabling businesses to maximize the potential of AI algorithms without the burden of specialized hardware or dedicated servers.

2. Empowering Real-Time Data Processing and Analysis:

One of the significant advantages of combining cloud computing and AI is the ability to process and analyze vast volumes of data in real-time. Cloud platforms offer the infrastructure necessary to store and process massive datasets securely. AI algorithms can then extract valuable insights and patterns from this data, enabling businesses to make informed decisions and optimize their operations based on up-to-date information. Real time data analysis empowers companies to respond quickly to market changes, customer demands, and emerging opportunities, leading to a competitive edge in the digital landscape.

3. Flexibility and Scalability for AI Workloads:

The cloud's inherent flexibility and scalability perfectly complement the computational requirements of AI. As the demand for computing resources fluctuates, cloud providers can dynamically allocate resources to handle AI workloads efficiently. This ensures that businesses can process data and run complex algorithms without experiencing performance issues or incurring excessive costs. The cloud's elasticity allows organizations to scale their AI operations seamlessly, regardless of the size and complexity of the workload. This scalability is crucial in enabling organizations to handle peak periods or sudden spikes in computational demands without compromising efficiency.

4. Enhanced Collaboration and Knowledge Sharing:

Cloud-based AI solutions foster collaboration and knowledge sharing within organizations. By leveraging the cloud, AI models and algorithms can be easily shared and deployed across multiple teams or departments. This streamlined collaboration results in more efficient workflows, accelerated development and deployment of AI solutions, and reduced duplication of efforts. The cloud becomes a central hub for storing, accessing, and collaborating on AI-related assets, enabling organizations to leverage collective intelligence and make faster progress. Additionally, cloud-based collaboration tools allow teams to connect and collaborate seamlessly, regardless of geographical locations, enhancing productivity and innovation.

5. Leveraging Pre-Trained Models and APIs:

Cloud computing offers businesses access to a wide range of pre-trained AI models and application programming interfaces (APIs). These models are trained on vast datasets and can perform complex tasks such as natural language processing, image recognition, and sentiment analysis. By tapping into these ready-to-use AI models and APIs, businesses can accelerate the adoption of AI capabilities and enhance their online services without starting from scratch. This reduces development time and costs while still delivering high-quality AI solutions. Furthermore, the availability of scalable infrastructure on the cloud enables businesses to train and fine-tune their own AI models, leveraging the power of distributed computing and cutting-edge frameworks.

6. Privacy and Security Considerations:

While the combination of cloud computing and AI brings numerous benefits, it also presents challenges and considerations. Data privacy and security are paramount concerns that must be addressed rigorously. Businesses must ensure that sensitive and confidential data is adequately protected when stored and processed in the cloud environment. Implementing robust encryption, access controls, and data governance policies becomes crucial to maintain the trust of customers and comply with regulations. Regular monitoring, auditing, and vulnerability assessments are essential practices to ensure the security and privacy of AI-powered applications and data.

7. Cost Optimization for AI Operations:

The cost implications of utilizing cloud resources for AI operations should be carefully evaluated to ensure that the benefits outweigh the expenses. While cloud services offer pay-as-you-go models, organizations must optimize their cloud usage to avoid overspending or underutilization. Adopting automated resource allocation, intelligent workload management, and implementing cost monitoring mechanisms can help strike a balance between cost-effectiveness and the computational requirements of AI workloads. Furthermore, cloud service providers often offer cost management tools and services to assist businesses in analyzing and optimizing their cloud spend, enabling them to make data-driven decisions and maximize the return on investment from their AI projects.

Conclusion:

In the digital age, the combination of cloud computing and AI provides a powerful synergy that enables businesses to thrive. By leveraging the inherent strengths of the cloud, organizations can harness the potential of AI to scale, optimize operations, and make data driven decisions. Cloud computing offers businesses the necessary infrastructure, flexibility, and scalability to process vast amounts of data, perform real-time analytics, and foster collaboration. However, businesses must also address challenges such as data privacy, security, and cost optimization. By carefully considering these factors and leveraging the capabilities of cloud computing and AI, businesses can unlock transformative opportunities, paving the way for a more intelligent and efficient future.

AI Profit: Harnessing Artificial Intelligence
For Online Wealth Creation

AI AND DIGITAL MARKETING: A NEW ERA

Digital marketing has gone through a significant transformation in recent years, primarily due to the advent of artificial intelligence (AI). AI, with its ability to analyze vast amounts of data and make intelligent predictions, has become a game-changer for marketers seeking to improve their marketing efforts and drive measurable growth.

In this chapter, we explore in greater depth the role of AI in digital marketing and how it is reshaping the landscape of online advertising, customer targeting, and campaign optimization. AI's remarkable capabilities allow marketers to achieve levels of personalization, efficiency, and effectiveness that were previously unimaginable.

One of the key ways AI is transforming digital marketing is through personalized experiences. By leveraging AI, marketers have the power to collect and analyze user data, enabling them to deliver highly tailored and relevant content to individual consumers. AI algorithms can process data from various sources, such as demographics, browsing behavior, purchase history, and social media activity, to create personalized advertisements, email campaigns, and website experiences. The result is a more intimate connection between businesses and consumers, leading to increased engagement, conversion rates, and brand loyalty.

Furthermore, AI plays an essential role in improving ad targeting. Traditional targeting methods often rely on basic user behavior or demographic information. However, AI algorithms can go beyond these parameters by analyzing a multitude of data points. By assessing factors like previous purchases, online preferences, search behavior, and social media interactions, AI can accurately identify individuals who are most likely to be interested in a brand's products or services. This level of precision enhances the effectiveness of advertising efforts, ensuring that marketing budgets are optimized and conversion rates are maximized.

In addition to personalization and ad targeting, AI is revolutionizing campaign optimization. AI-powered tools can analyze campaign performance in real-time, providing marketers with insights previously inaccessible. By monitoring metrics like click-through rates, cost-per-acquisition, and return on ad spend, AI can identify trends and patterns that human marketers may overlook. This allows for data-driven decision making and enables marketers to optimize their strategies accordingly. Whether it's adjusting ad spend, testing different creative variations, or optimizing landing pages, AI provides marketers with the actionable insights needed to continuously improve campaign performance and achieve better results.

However, as AI continues to advance and play a more prominent role in digital marketing, ethical considerations must be taken into account. Marketers must ensure that they are employing AI algorithms responsibly and ethically. Transparency is crucial, as consumers should be informed about how their data is being used and have control over their privacy. Respecting consumer trust and privacy is essential to building lasting relationships with customers and maintaining a positive brand image.

As we delve deeper into this new era of AI-powered digital marketing, it becomes evident that the impact of AI on online advertising is significant. By embracing AI tools and techniques, marketers can leverage the power of data and automation to create highly targeted, personalized campaigns that drive meaningful engagement and deliver exceptional results.

In the next chapter, we will explore the practical applications of AI tools for customer relationship management (CRM) and how businesses can revolutionize the way they manage and nurture their customer relationships using AI-powered CRM systems.

AI Profit: Harnessing Artificial Intelligence
For Online Wealth Creation

———

USING AI TOOLS FOR CUSTOMER RELATIONSHIP MANAGEMENT

In today's highly competitive business landscape, maintaining strong relationships with customers is crucial for sustainable success. While traditional customer relationship management (CRM) systems have been effective in managing customer data and interactions, the integration of AI tools has taken CRM to a whole new level.

AI-powered CRM tools harness the capabilities of artificial intelligence and machine learning to analyze vast amounts of customer data, identify patterns, and predict customer behavior. This allows businesses to gain detailed insights into customer sentiment, preferences, and purchasing habits, enabling them to personalize their marketing efforts and provide exceptional customer experiences.

One of the key benefits of using AI tools for CRM is the ability to automate repetitive tasks which were once time-consuming for sales and customer service teams. For example, AI chatbots can handle routine customer queries and provide real-time support, ensuring faster response times and improving customer satisfaction. These chatbots can identify customer intent and provide accurate and personalized responses, making customers feel valued and understood.

AI tools also enable businesses to segment their customer base effectively. By analyzing customer data and identifying common characteristics, AI-powered CRM systems can help businesses create targeted marketing campaigns. For instance, AI algorithms can group customers based on demographics, purchasing behavior, or preferences, allowing businesses to tailor their offerings and messages accordingly. This level of personalization not only increases the effectiveness of marketing efforts but also strengthens customer loyalty and engagement.

Furthermore, AI tools can assist in lead generation and conversion. By analyzing historical data and identifying patterns indicative of potential customers, AI-powered CRM systems can provide valuable insights and recommendations on leads that are most likely to convert. This allows sales teams to prioritize their efforts effectively, maximizing their chances of closing deals.

In addition, AI tools can improve the accuracy and efficiency of sales forecasts. By analyzing historical sales data, market trends, customer behavior, and external factors, AI powered CRM systems can generate accurate and reliable sales forecasts. These forecasts enable businesses to make informed decisions, allocate resources effectively, and identify potential obstacles or opportunities in the market.

Moreover, AI tools can offer proactive customer service by identifying and resolving issues before they become problems. Through sentiment analysis and natural language processing, AI-powered CRM systems can analyze customer feedback and detect potential dissatisfaction or emerging issues. This allows businesses to intervene promptly, address concerns, and enhance customer experiences. By proactively addressing customer needs and resolving issues in a timely manner, businesses can strengthen customer loyalty and improve customer retention.

Another area where AI tools are revolutionizing CRM is in the field of predictive analytics. By analyzing historical customer data, including buying behavior, purchasing frequency, and product preferences, AI-powered CRM systems can predict customer churn, identify cross selling and upselling opportunities, and even provide recommendations for personalized offerings. This level of personalization not only enhances customer satisfaction but also increases the chances of repeat purchases and brand loyalty.

Additionally, AI tools can assist in social media monitoring and management. By analyzing social media conversations, sentiment, and engagement, AI-powered CRM systems enable businesses to monitor brand reputation, identify influencers, and even detect potential crisis situations. This real-time monitoring allows companies to respond swiftly, manage their online presence effectively, and nurture positive customer relationships.

However, while AI tools provide numerous benefits for CRM, it is important to balance them with the need for human touch. While AI can automate processes and enhance efficiency, human interactions still hold significant value, especially in building relationships and providing personalized experiences. Finding the right balance between AI-driven automation and human interaction is key to successful CRM implementation.

In conclusion, using AI tools for customer relationship management has become essential for businesses seeking to thrive in today's digital age. These tools provide detailed insights into customer data, automate repetitive tasks, enhance personalization efforts, and improve overall customer satisfaction. By leveraging the power of AI, businesses can streamline their CRM processes, drive growth, and gain a competitive edge in the market.

This synergy between AI and CRM opens up new possibilities for businesses to forge stronger and more meaningful relationships with their customers, ultimately leading to long term success.

AI Profit: Harnessing Artificial Intelligence
For Online Wealth Creation

———

CASE STUDIES: AI IN CUSTOMER RELATIONSHIP MANAGEMENT

Introduction:

In this book where we delve deeper into the fascinating world of AI in customer relationship management (CRM). In this chapter, we will explore a comprehensive range of real-life case studies that showcase the profound and transformative impact of AI on CRM strategies. Through these in-depth examples, we'll gain a deeper understanding of how AI has revolutionized customer relationship management, providing valuable insights, enhancing the overall customer experience, and ultimately, fostering stronger customer loyalty.

Case Study 1: ABC Bank

ABC Bank, a leading financial institution, embarked on a digital transformation of their customer service operations by implementing AI-powered CRM software. This innovative solution employed powerful machine learning algorithms to analyze vast amounts of customer data including transactions, interactions, and demographic information. By leveraging AI, ABC Bank effectively detected patterns and trends in customer behavior, preferences, and financial needs.

These valuable insights empowered ABC Bank to personalize their marketing campaigns and offer tailored financial products to targeted customer segments. By reaching out to customers with personalized recommendations and offers, ABC Bank experienced a significant increase in customer engagement and conversion rates. Moreover, the AI system implemented real-time customer support features, such as AI-powered chatbots, enabling ABC Bank to engage with customers instantaneously and provide prompt assistance.

As a result, ABC Bank witnessed a substantial boost in revenue, significantly improved customer satisfaction ratings, and a higher rate of customer loyalty. The implementation of AI in their CRM strategies not only enhanced their competitive position in the financial industry but also solidified their position as a trusted and customer-centric financial institution.

Case Study 2: XYZ Retail

In the highly competitive e-commerce industry, XYZ Retail sought a significant edge by integrating AI into their CRM strategies. By leveraging advanced AI algorithms, XYZ Retail analyzed vast amounts of customer data, including browsing habits, purchase history, and preferences. This comprehensive analysis provided XYZ Retail with invaluable insights into each customer's preferences, interests, and buying patterns.

Utilizing these insights, the CRM system enabled XYZ Retail to offer highly personalized product recommendations, tailored promotions, and discounts for individual customers. By providing a unique and customized shopping experience, XYZ Retail experienced exceptional conversion rates, improved customer engagement, and consequently, sustained business growth.

Moreover, AI-powered chatbots were employed on XYZ Retail's website to assist customers with queries in real-time, enhancing the overall shopping experience and reducing customer frustration. These chatbots utilized natural language processing and deep learning techniques to understand customer inquiries and provide accurate and timely responses.

Through the implementation of AI in their CRM strategies, XYZ Retail established a reputation for personalized service and reinforced customer loyalty. This success, in turn, translated into increased customer retention, improved customer lifetime value (CLV), and enhanced profitability for the company.

Case Study 3: DEF Airlines

DEF Airlines, a prominent player in the global airline industry, recognized the importance of enhancing customer service and loyalty. To achieve this, they embraced AI-powered CRM solutions. By leveraging AI algorithms, DEF Airlines conducted comprehensive analyses of customer feedback, preferences, and travel history. This allowed them to provide personalized travel recommendations, customize rewards based on individual preferences, and offer an enhanced overall travel experience.

AI proved particularly powerful in predicting potential flight delays and cancellations. The AI system analyzed historical flight data, weather conditions, air traffic patterns, and other relevant factors to accurately forecast potential disruptions. Armed with this information, DEF Airlines was able to proactively communicate with customers, informing them of any potential flight changes and providing alternative solutions. This proactive approach served to minimize inconvenience to customers and bolstered their overall satisfaction.

Furthermore, the AI-powered CRM system enabled DEF Airlines to personalize their interactions with customers. This personalization extended to targeted marketing campaigns, personalized promotions, and tailored offerings that resonated with individual customers. By leveraging AI to strengthen their CRM strategies, DEF Airlines witnessed remarkable improvements in customer satisfaction, leading to an impressive increase in customer loyalty, and consequently, a substantial boost in revenue and market share.

Case Study 4: GHI Telecom

GHI Telecom, a leading telecommunications provider, recognized that customer support plays a crucial role in their industry. To optimize their customer service capabilities, GHI Telecom integrated AI into their CRM systems. By employing AI-powered chatbots and virtual assistants, GHI Telecom was able to provide immediate and accurate responses to customer inquiries, significantly improving the overall customer experience.

The AI system harnessed natural language processing and deep learning algorithms to understand customer requests, provide relevant information, and resolve issues promptly. This AI-powered assistance empowered GHI Telecom's customers with instant responses to their queries, eliminating the need for prolonged wait times or repetitive interactions with human agents.

Moreover, the AI system continuously analyzed customer sentiment, detecting potential issues, and flagging them for prompt attention. This proactive approach allowed GHI Telecom to address concerns swiftly, improve service quality, and ultimately enhance customer satisfaction. By optimizing their customer support capabilities through AI, GHI Telecom observed a remarkable increase in customer satisfaction ratings, a decrease in customer churn, and a substantial improvement in their overall business performance.

Conclusion:

These comprehensive case studies provide compelling evidence of the transformative impact of AI in customer relationship management. By leveraging the power of AI technologies, businesses can gain valuable insights, improve customer service, increase customer loyalty, and drive sustainable growth. As AI continues to evolve, its potential within CRM strategies will only amplify. Consequently, businesses that embrace this technological revolution will thrive in the digital age as they build stronger and more meaningful relationships with their customers, establishing a competitive edge in their respective industries. Through the integration of AI into CRM strategies, businesses are poised to unlock new levels of success and customer-centricity in the years to come.

AI Profit: Harnessing Artificial Intelligence
For Online Wealth Creation

AI AND CYBERSECURITY: PROTECTING YOUR ONLINE BUSINESS

Introduction:

In today's digital landscape, the prevalence of online businesses has soared, bringing with it increased concerns regarding cybersecurity. The rapid evolution of cyber threats, ranging from sophisticated ransomware attacks to social engineering scams, requires organizations to adopt advanced measures to safeguard their digital assets. Artificial Intelligence (AI) has emerged as a potent ally in this battle, with its ability to analyze vast amounts of data and adapt to changing threat landscapes. This extended chapter delves deeper into the intersection of AI and cybersecurity, exploring various applications, benefits, and emerging trends that harness the power of AI to protect online businesses.

1. Analyzing Massive Data Sets in Real-Time:

AI algorithms possess the capability to process and analyze massive volumes of data in real-time, enabling organizations to gain valuable insights while minimizing response times. AI-powered systems monitor network traffic, examining intricate patterns, and flagged anomalies that may signify a potential cybersecurity breach. By employing machine learning algorithms, AI can quickly learn from past incidents and proactively identify indicators of compromise, thus enhancing the accuracy and efficiency of threat detection.

a) Data Analysis and Predictive Analytics: AI can leverage predictive analytics to identify potential vulnerabilities and predict future threats based on historical and real-time data. By assimilating massive data sets from various sources, AI algorithms can identify patterns and predict potential attack vectors or vulnerabilities. Predictive analytics helps organizations stay one step ahead of cybercriminals, enabling them to proactively implement security measures and defend against emerging threats.

b) Behavioral Analysis: AI excels in behavioral analysis, studying user patterns, and identifying anomalous behaviors that deviate from established norms. By analyzing user behavior, such as login patterns, access behavior, and data requests, AI systems can detect suspicious activities and trigger alerts or additional authentication measures. This proactive approach strengthens the access control mechanisms, minimizing the risk of unauthorized access and identity theft.

2. Advanced Threat Detection and Prevention:

Traditional cybersecurity measures often fall short in rapidly identifying and thwarting advanced and persistent threats. Conversely, AI systems demonstrate adaptability and agility, enabling them to continuously learn from new attack patterns and techniques. This capacity positions AI as a paramount tool for advanced threat detection and prevention.

a) Machine Learning Algorithms: AI systems leverage machine learning algorithms to identify patterns and behaviors associated with cyber-attacks. Through continuous learning, AI models gain expertise in distinguishing legitimate activities from malicious ones, helping organizations identify and mitigate threats more effectively. Machine learning enables AI systems to adapt and evolve in response to new cyber threats, ensuring businesses stay resilient in the face of emerging challenges.

b) Deep Learning and Neural Networks: Deep learning, a subset of AI, utilizes neural networks to process complex data sets and detect patterns that a human observer might overlook. This technology is particularly suited for cybersecurity, as it can identify novel attack methods and recognize subtle variations in cyber threats. By training neural networks with vast amounts of data, organizations can equip AI-powered systems with a high level of accuracy and precision in threat detection.

3. User Authentication and Access Control:

Ensuring secure user authentication is of paramount importance for safeguarding online businesses. AI plays a vital role in strengthening access control measures, minimizing the risk of unauthorized access, and protecting sensitive information.

a) Multi-Factor Authentication (MFA): AI-powered systems can integrate MFA techniques, strengthening the authentication process beyond traditional username and password combinations. By analyzing user behavior, device information, and biometric data, AI can determine the authenticity of user access attempts. MFA systems powered by AI can swiftly identify suspicious login attempts and request additional verification methods like fingerprint scanning, facial recognition, or SMS verification codes.

b) Contextual Authentication: Contextual authentication involves analyzing multiple variables, including user behavior, geolocation, and device characteristics, to assess the authenticity of login attempts. AI systems employ machine learning algorithms to learn, adapt, and distinguish normal user behavior from malicious activities. This dynamic approach ensures enhanced security by enabling the system to prompt additional verification measures when unusual access patterns are detected.

4. Incident Response and Mitigation:

In the unfortunate event of a security breach, organizations must respond swiftly and effectively to minimize damage and disruption. AI plays a vital role in automating incident response and mitigation processes, improving response times, and reducing recovery costs.

a) Automated Incident Analysis: AI-powered security systems can automatically analyze security incidents, categorize their severity, and prioritize response based on potential impact and risk. By quickly identifying affected systems and determining the extent of compromise, AI assists in focused incident management, allowing security teams to allocate resources efficiently and minimize recovery times.

b) Threat Intelligence and Predictive Response: AI systems aid in generating actionable threat intelligence reports, providing insights into emerging threats and vulnerabilities. By analyzing vast amounts of threat data from various sources, AI can equip organizations with real-time threat intelligence, enabling proactive defense and response strategies. Predictive response capabilities also empower organizations to anticipate potential threats, deploy patches, and strengthen their cybersecurity defenses in advance.

5. Challenges and Ethical Considerations:

While AI brings significant advantages to cybersecurity,

organizations must navigate challenges and ethical considerations to ensure the effectiveness and integrity of their cybersecurity defenses.

a) Continuous Learning and Adaptation: AI models in cybersecurity require constant updates and training to adapt to evolving threats. Organizations must prioritize ongoing investments in AI technologies, including regular updates to threat intelligence databases, ensuring that AI systems contend with the latest attack vectors.

b) Data Privacy and Security: AI-powered cybersecurity systems rely on analyzing vast amounts of data for effective detection and prevention. It is crucial for organizations to implement robust data protection measures, safeguarding the privacy and integrity of sensitive information. Encryption, access control, and comprehensive data management practices should be embraced to maintain user trust and comply with stringent data protection guidelines.

c) Transparency and Explainability: To foster user trust and ensure accountability, organizations should prioritize transparency in AI implementation. Accessible explanations of how AI algorithms work, the data sources they utilize, and how they arrive at decisions enhance trust among users and foster greater transparency in cybersecurity practices.

Conclusion:

Artificial Intelligence has emerged as a powerful tool in bolstering cybersecurity defenses for online businesses. Its ability to analyze massive data sets, swiftly detect anomalies, and adapt to changing threat landscapes provides organizations with a proactive approach to protect their valuable assets. By leveraging AI for advanced threat detection, user authentication, incident response, and predictive analytics, businesses can significantly reduce the risk of security breaches and ensure robust cybersecurity measures. It is important, however, for organizations to address challenges such as continuous learning, data privacy, and transparency, in order to maximize the benefits of AI while maintaining trust and ethical standards.

AI Profit: Harnessing Artificial Intelligence
For Online Wealth Creation

———

THE FUTURE OF AI IN ONLINE BUSINESS

The future of AI in online business is a fascinating terrain ripe with potential and innovation. As technology continues to evolve at an unprecedented pace, artificial intelligence has emerged as a key driver of transformation within the online business landscape. This chapter delves deeper into the profound impact AI is set to have on various aspects of online business, exploring personalized customer experiences, automation, data analytics, cybersecurity, and the ethical considerations associated with AI implementation.

Personalized customer experiences hold tremendous promise in the future of AI-powered online business. Through sophisticated algorithms and machine learning capabilities, businesses can analyze vast amounts of customer data to derive meaningful insights and craft personalized recommendations. From tailored advertising to customized product offerings, AI can elevate customer satisfaction levels by delivering highly relevant and targeted experiences. This shift towards personalization not only cultivates stronger customer engagement and loyalty but also generates higher conversion rates and increased brand advocacy. With the aid of AI, businesses can create seamless customer journeys, anticipating their needs and preferences, and offering tailored solutions in real time. This capability has the potential to revolutionize the way businesses interact with their customers, creating lasting relationships built on understanding and trust.

Automation is another vital area where AI will reshape the landscape of online business. By harnessing the power of AI, businesses can automate repetitive and time-consuming tasks, effectively freeing up human resources to focus on more strategic endeavors. Chatbots, for instance, equipped with Natural Language Processing (NLP) capabilities, can effectively handle customer queries and support, ensuring prompt and accurate responses. These AI powered chatbots can simulate human-like conversations, providing users with a seamless and efficient experience. Additionally, AI can streamline various backend operations such as inventory management, order processing, and supply chain logistics, optimizing efficiency and reducing costs. The use of robotic process automation (RPA) in conjunction with AI can further enhance automation capabilities, leading to increased productivity and scalability for online businesses.

Data analytics stands as a cornerstone in the future of AI-driven online business. With the ability to process and analyze vast amounts of data, AI algorithms can discover hidden patterns and trends that may elude human analysis. By providing valuable insights and actionable intelligence, businesses can make data-driven decisions with greater precision and confidence. AI-powered analytics offer valuable competitive advantages, enabling businesses to identify emerging trends, forecast market demand, and optimize pricing and product strategies. Moreover, AI enhances the potential of predictive analytics, enabling businesses to anticipate customer behavior and tailor their offerings accordingly, further driving customer satisfaction and business performance. With AI, businesses can gain a holistic view of their operations, identifying opportunities for improvement, and making informed decisions to stay ahead of the competition.

In the realm of cybersecurity, AI is set to reshape defense mechanisms against online threats. As the digital landscape becomes increasingly complex, businesses face growing challenges in safeguarding their assets and customer data. AI-powered cybersecurity systems can continuously monitor networks, detect potential vulnerabilities, and swiftly respond to emerging cyberattacks. These systems employ machine learning algorithms to learn from new threats and adapt their defenses accordingly. By employing AI in cybersecurity, businesses can proactively protect their online infrastructure, ensuring data integrity and customer trust. AI can assist in threat detection by analyzing patterns and anomalies in network traffic, identifying potential risks before they escalate. It can further support incident response by providing real-time insights and automating remediation efforts. With AI, businesses can fortify their cybersecurity posture and reduce the impact of cyber threats.

Despite the immense potential of AI in online business, ethical considerations must be at the forefront of its implementation. As AI becomes more integrated into daily operations, it raises concerns about privacy, bias, and accountability. Businesses must ensure transparent and ethical practices in their utilization of AI technology. By prioritizing ethical AI guidelines and regulations, businesses can mitigate the risks associated with biased decision-making, ingrained prejudices, and unauthorized use of personal data. Collaboration between governments, industry leaders, and experts is necessary to establish industry standards that reflect responsible and ethical use of AI in online business. Companies must also be mindful of the potential consequences of AI misuse, such as unemployment or job displacement, and actively work towards solutions that leverage AI to empower human workers rather than replace them. It is crucial to strike a balance between the efficiency and convenience offered by AI and the fundamental values of fairness, transparency, and inclusivity.

In conclusion, the future of AI in online business promises a revolution in personalized customer experiences, automation, data analytics, and cybersecurity. Through AI-powered personalization, businesses can establish deeper connections with customers, driving higher engagement and loyalty. Automation enhances efficiency by delegating routine tasks to AI, allowing human resources to focus on strategic initiatives. Data analytics enables businesses to unlock powerful insights, empowering data-driven decision-making. Additionally, AI enhances cybersecurity defenses, bolstering protection against online threats. By embracing AI ethically, businesses can unleash the full potential of this transformative technology, fostering sustainable growth and success in the online business landscape of the future. The future of online business is one where AI acts as a trusted partner, augmenting human capabilities and enabling businesses to thrive in an increasingly digital world.

AI Profit: Harnessing Artificial Intelligence
For Online Wealth Creation

ETHICAL CONSIDERATIONS IN AI

Introduction:

Artificial Intelligence (AI) has emerged as a transformative technology with immense potential in various fields. While AI offers numerous benefits, it also raises significant ethical considerations that must be addressed to ensure responsible and fair deployment. This chapter delves into the core ethical considerations surrounding AI, including bias, human labor impact, transparency, privacy, data protection, misuse, and social impact. By exploring and understanding these ethical dimensions, we can navigate the complex landscape of AI and foster its positive impact on society.

Section 1: Bias in AI

Bias in AI poses a significant ethical concern as it can perpetuate and amplify societal inequalities. AI algorithms are trained on vast datasets, which can inadvertently contain biases present in society. If these biases are not identified and corrected, AI systems may produce discriminatory outcomes, reinforcing societal prejudices. It is crucial for developers and users of AI to actively work towards identifying and mitigating bias, employing fairness metrics and comprehensive evaluation processes.

Subsection 1.1: Algorithmic Bias

Algorithmic bias refers to the skew in AI systems' decision-making processes due to biased training data or the influence of implicit societal biases. For example, facial recognition algorithms have demonstrated higher error rates for people of color, women, and elderly individuals due to underrepresentation in training data. Addressing algorithmic bias requires diverse and inclusive datasets, rigorous testing, and ongoing monitoring to reduce unfair outcomes and ensure equitable AI systems.

Subsubsection 1.1.1: Types of Bias in AI

Bias in AI can manifest in various forms, including:
1.1.1.1 Selection Bias: Occurs when the training dataset is not representative of the entire population, leading to biased decision-making.

1.1.1.2 Confirmation Bias: Arises when AI algorithms reinforce existing beliefs or stereotypes, without considering contradictory evidence.

1.1.1.3 Sampling Bias: Results from a non-random subset of data being used for training, leading to skewed results.

1.1.1.4 Prejudicial Bias: Occurs when the AI system explicitly discriminates against a specific group based on attributes such as race, gender, or age.

Subsection 1.2: Data Bias

Data bias occurs when the data used to train AI models reflects societal biases, leading to discriminatory results. Biased data can reinforce stereotypes or exclude marginalized groups. It is essential to be mindful of the source, quality, and representativeness of training data and to implement data collection strategies that gather diverse perspectives. Appropriate data preprocessing techniques and evaluation methods should be employed to minimize bias and promote fairness.

Subsubsection 1.2.1: Proxy Bias

Proxy biases arise when indirect factors present in training data correlate with certain attributes and unintentionally lead to biased outcomes. For example, if an AI system is trained on data where male pronouns are frequently associated with high-paying job titles, it may automatically associate males with higher professional competence, perpetuating gender bias.

Subsubsection 1.2.2: Correcting Data Bias

Correcting data bias requires a combination of careful dataset curation, feature engineering, and algorithmic techniques. Creating a diverse and representative dataset helps in capturing different perspectives and avoiding discriminatory outcomes. Additionally, debiasing algorithms, such as the use of fairness-aware learning, can help correct biases and minimize unfairness in AI systems.

Section 2: Impact on Human Labor

The increasing integration of AI technologies raises concerns about the potential displacement of human workers and the exacerbation of economic inequality. While AI can enhance efficiency and productivity, it also has the potential to replace certain job roles, leading to job loss in various sectors. Ethical considerations surrounding human labor in AI include ensuring appropriate reskilling and upskilling opportunities, implementing strategies for job creation, and designing AI systems that augment human capabilities rather than replacing them entirely.

Subsection 2.1: Job Loss vs. Job Creation

As AI systems automate certain tasks, there is a valid concern over job loss, particularly in industries heavily reliant on routine tasks. However, history has shown that technological advancements often create new job opportunities. Therefore, it is essential to focus on job creation in emerging AI-driven fields and actively invest in reskilling and upskilling initiatives to facilitate the smooth transition of workers into new roles. Additionally, ethical considerations should account for potential economic disparities caused by AI-driven job polarization.

Subsubsection 2.1.1: Addressing Job Displacement

To address job displacement, governments, organizations, and educational institutions need to collaborate in reskilling and upskilling the workforce. Providing accessible and affordable training programs that enable individuals to acquire new skills relevant to the AI-dominated job market is crucial. Emphasizing the development of uniquely human capabilities, such as
creativity, critical thinking, emotional intelligence, and complex problem-solving, can help individuals thrive alongside AI technologies.

Subsubsection 2.1.2: Redefining Work and Automation

Beyond job creation and reskilling efforts, redefining the concept of work itself becomes important in the AI era. Exploring alternative models like universal basic income, shorter workweeks, or job sharing can help distribute the benefits of automation more equitably.
Redefining work allows society to reimagine the value of human labor and build a future where AI augments human potential rather than replacing it.

Section 3: Transparency and Explainability

Transparency and explainability are critical ethical considerations in AI. Many AI systems, such as deep learning models, often operate as "black boxes," making it challenging to understand and interpret their decision-making processes. This lack of transparency raises

concerns about accountability, social acceptance, and the potential for biased or unjust outcomes. Efforts should be directed towards developing AI systems that are transparent, explainable, and auditable, allowing users and stakeholders to understand, challenge, and correct any potential errors or biases.

Subsection 3.1: Explainable AI

Explainable AI (XAI) aims to enable humans to comprehend and trust AI systems' decision making processes. By providing interpretability, XAI techniques allow stakeholders to understand how AI arrives at its conclusions, ensuring transparency and accountability. Developing robust XAI methodologies involves integrating human-understandable rules, visualizations, and explanations into AI systems, enabling users to grasp the underlying factors contributing to AI-generated outcomes.

Subsubsection 3.1.1: Model Transparency

Model transparency involves providing visibility into AI models' inner workings, making them understandable and auditable. Techniques such as rule-based models, decision trees, and symbolic representations can enhance transparency by offering clear rules and explanations behind the AI system's decisions. Transparency not only aids in addressing bias but also helps build trust among users and stakeholders.

Subsubsection 3.1.2: Interpreting Neural Networks

Interpreting complex neural networks, such as deep learning models, is a significant challenge in XAI. Methods like layer-wise relevance propagation, saliency maps, and attention mechanisms help highlight important input features and provide insights into how the AI system processes information. Improving the interpretability of neural networks contributes to transparency and enables users to challenge or question the decisions made by these models.

Subsection 3.2: Bias Identification and Mitigation

Transparency is crucial for identifying and addressing bias in AI systems. Ethical considerations demand proactive efforts to recognize and mitigate biases, ensuring fair decision-making. Techniques like fairness-aware learning, adversarial debiasing, and counterfactual fairness can help identify and reduce bias in AI systems. Additionally, comprehensive evaluation methodologies should be implemented to assess the fairness and equity of AI systems throughout their development and deployment stages.

Subsubsection 3.2.1: Fairness Metrics

Fairness metrics play a vital role in evaluating AI system performance and assessing the fairness of decision outcomes. Metrics like demographic parity, equalized odds, and equal opportunity measure the disparate impact of AI systems across different groups and help identify instances of bias. By incorporating fairness metrics into AI development processes, bias can be systematically identified and mitigated.

Subsubsection 3.2.2: Auditing and Certification

Regular auditing and certification processes can ensure that AI systems comply with ethical standards. Independent organizations and regulatory bodies can perform audits to evaluate AI systems' performance in terms of fairness, transparency, and accountability. Certification processes can provide third-party validation and establish trust among users and stakeholders, fostering responsible AI deployment.

Section 4: Privacy and Data Protection

AI systems heavily rely on vast amounts of data, raising concerns regarding privacy and data protection. Ethical considerations demand that AI development and deployment prioritize safeguarding individuals' privacy rights and ensuring the responsible handling of personal data. Policies, regulations, and technical measures should be in place to protect user privacy, promote data anonymization, and obtain informed consent for data usage.

Subsection 4.1: Data Privacy

Data privacy involves protecting individuals' sensitive information from unauthorized access or use. AI systems often collect and process personal data, and it is essential to prioritize privacy throughout the entire data lifecycle. Privacy-enhancing technologies, secure data storage, data minimization techniques, and strict access controls can help safeguard individuals' privacy while utilizing data for AI development and training.

Subsubsection 4.1.1: Privacy by Design

Privacy by Design is an ethical principle that emphasizes the integration of privacy considerations into the early stages of AI system development. Privacy should be addressed proactively, ensuring that AI systems are designed with privacy-preserving mechanisms by default. Implementing privacy-enhancing techniques, such as data anonymization, differential privacy, and secure multiparty computation, can help protect individuals' privacy rights.

Subsubsection 4.1.2: Consent and Data Usage

Informed consent and transparency are crucial when collecting and using personal data for AI purposes. Ethical considerations require that individuals understand and consent to the collection and use of their data. Providing clear explanations about the purpose, scope, and potential risks of data usage can empower individuals to make informed decisions and maintain control over their data.

Subsection 4.2: Algorithmic Privacy

Algorithmic privacy refers to the protection of individuals' data and information during the training and inference processes of AI systems. AI algorithms should be designed to prevent unauthorized access or disclosure of sensitive data. Techniques like federated learning, secure multiparty computation, and homomorphic encryption enable collaborative data analysis while preserving privacy and data confidentiality.

Subsubsection 4.2.1: Differential Privacy

Differential privacy is a technique that aims to protect individuals' privacy when analyzing aggregate data. By adding appropriate noise or perturbation to aggregated results, differential privacy ensures that individual data points cannot be re-identified. Implementing differential privacy mechanisms in AI systems helps balance the utility of data analysis with privacy protection.

Subsubsection 4.2.2: Secure Data Sharing

Secure data sharing techniques enable collaboration and information exchange while protecting privacy. Methods like secure multi-party computation allow multiple parties to jointly compute results without revealing their individual inputs. Secure data sharing mechanisms foster responsible data sharing practices, making it possible to leverage collective intelligence without compromising privacy.

Section 5: Misuse and Unintended Consequences

AI technologies can be misused, leading to harmful outcomes and significant ethical concerns. It is crucial to consider the potential negative consequences of AI systems and ensure safeguards against misuse. Responsible AI development and deployment should incorporate ethical guidelines, regulatory frameworks, and ongoing monitoring to mitigate the risks of AI misuse and unintended consequences.

Subsection 5.1: Adversarial Attacks

Adversarial attacks involve intentionally manipulating AI systems to produce incorrect or malicious outputs. Adversaries can exploit vulnerabilities in AI algorithms to deceive or manipulate AI systems, leading to potentially harmful consequences. Ethical considerations demand developing robust defense mechanisms against adversarial attacks, including adversarial training, detection techniques, and safeguards to ensure AI system resilience.

Subsubsection 5.1.1: Robustness and Security

Enhancing AI system robustness and security is crucial to prevent misuse and adversarial attacks. Techniques like input sanitization, anomaly detection, and model hardening can help mitigate vulnerabilities and safeguard AI systems against malicious manipulation. Regular updates, security audits, and responsible disclosure practices contribute to AI system resilience and protect against potential misuse.

Subsubsection 5.1.2: Responsible Disclosure

Responsible disclosure practices involve actively reporting and addressing vulnerabilities or weaknesses in AI systems. Researchers, developers, and users should collaborate to identify and fix security flaws, ensuring the responsible use of AI technologies. Promoting a culture of responsible disclosure encourages transparency, accountability, and the continual improvement of AI system security.

Subsection 5.2: Unintended Consequences

AI systems can have unintended consequences, resulting from unforeseen biases, errors, or unintended uses. Responsible AI development requires comprehensive testing, evaluation, and ongoing monitoring to identify and mitigate these unintended consequences. Ethical considerations demand that developers and users proactively address potential harms and continuously refine AI systems to minimize negative impacts on individuals and society as a whole.

Subsubsection 5.2.1: Ethical Risk Assessment

Ethical risk assessment involves identifying and analyzing the ethical implications associated with AI technologies. Assessing potential risks and unintended consequences early in the development process enables proactive mitigation strategies. Ethical risk assessment frameworks can guide developers and organizations in identifying, analyzing, and addressing ethical concerns related to AI deployments.

Subsubsection 5.2.2: Continuous Monitoring and Improvement

Continuous monitoring and improvement of AI systems are essential to address emerging ethical concerns and adapt to changing societal needs. Regular evaluation, feedback loops, and user engagement allow for the identification of potential issues and the refinement of AI systems. Ongoing monitoring fosters responsible AI deployment and helps ensure that the technology evolves in a manner that aligns with ethical considerations and societal values.

Conclusion:

Ethical considerations play a fundamental role in the development, deployment, and use of AI technologies. Addressing bias, ensuring the impact on human labor, promoting transparency and explainability, safeguarding privacy and data protection, mitigating misuse and unintended consequences are critical for establishing responsible AI practices. By incorporating these ethical dimensions, society can harness the potential of AI while safeguarding against potential harm and promoting fairness, equity, accountability, and respect for individual and collective well-being.

AI Profit: Harnessing Artificial Intelligence
For Online Wealth Creation

FINAL THOUGHTS: EMBRACING AI FOR ONLINE WEALTH CREATION

As we come to the end of this transformative journey exploring the potential of AI for online wealth creation, it is crucial to reflect on the key takeaways and conclude with final thoughts that offer deeper insights into this dynamic field.

Entrepreneurship in the age of AI has become an endeavor interwoven with technology, innovation, and a deep understanding of AI-driven opportunities. In this final chapter, we celebrate the incredible possibilities that arise when entrepreneurs and innovators harness the power of AI in their online ventures. With a light touch, we offer reflections and parting thoughts to guide you on your continued path towards leveraging AI for online wealth creation.

1. The Expanding Scope of AI-Driven Entrepreneurship:

We have witnessed how AI opens doors to new business models, revenue streams, and customer experiences. As we part ways, it is important to recognize the expanding scope of AI-driven entrepreneurship. Gone are the days when business acumen was the sole requirement for success. Today, entrepreneurs need to develop a thorough understanding of AI technologies and cultivate a technology-driven mindset. By nurturing a culture of innovation and encouraging experimentation, entrepreneurs can embrace AI-driven entrepreneurship fully.

2. Augmenting Human Intelligence: A Symphony of Minds:

One of the most beautiful aspects of AI lies in its ability to amplify and augment human intelligence rather than replace it. AI is not a competition but a creative collaboration, a symphony of minds. In this section, we explore how AI can empower individuals to take their online businesses to new heights. By providing actionable insights, automating repetitive tasks, and freeing up precious time, AI enables entrepreneurs to focus on critical decision making, creativity, and problem-solving. Embrace AI as a partner in amplifying your intellectual capabilities.

3. Ethical AI for Sustainable Success:

As AI continues to shape the landscape of online wealth creation, ethical considerations become paramount. We cannot talk about fostering prosperity without addressing the need for ethical AI practices. In this section, we delve into the importance of integrating ethical AI principles into every aspect of your business operations. From mitigating biases and ensuring data privacy to fostering inclusivity and transparency, ethical AI paves the path to sustainable success. Let your business be guided by ethical AI practices that prioritize fairness, accountability, and the greater good.

4. Scaling and Future-Proofing Strategies for Enduring Success:

As you integrate AI into your online wealth creation endeavors, scalability and future proofing become essential considerations. In this section, we dive into strategies for seamlessly integrating AI into your business. Build scalable infrastructure that can accommodate increasing AI-driven demands. Design flexible AI models that can adapt to evolving needs and technological advancements. Stay updated with emerging AI trends and continuously learn to refine your AI strategy. Collaboration and openness to change are key to scaling and future-proofing your business.

5. Embracing a Global Perspective:

The rise of online businesses has the power to transcend geographical boundaries, connecting businesses with audiences worldwide. In this section, we emphasize the importance of embracing a global perspective in your AI-driven online ventures. Leverage AI for localization, personalization, and cross-cultural understanding. Tailoring your online business to resonate with diverse international audiences unlocks new avenues of growth and establishes a strong global presence. Embrace the richness of global diversity and cater to the unique needs of each market.

6. Life-Long Learning and Adaptability in the AI Era:

Our final thoughts center around the need for life-long learning and adaptability in the fast-paced AI-driven world. As AI advancements continue to accelerate, it is essential to stay informed, curious, and supported by a continuous learning mindset. Actively participate in industry conferences, engage with professional networks, and explore collaboration opportunities. Embrace a growth mindset that encourages embracing emerging technologies, and continuously adapt your business to seize new AI-driven opportunities. The only constant in the AI era is change, and your ability to adapt will be the key to your success.

In closing, we hope that this comprehensive exploration of AI for online wealth creation has ignited your imagination, provided you with practical insights, and instilled a sense of excitement as you embark on your journey towards leveraging AI for success. Embrace the possibilities that AI offers, champion ethical practices, and align your business with the positive social impact that AI can bring. By doing so, you can shape a prosperous and sustainable future by combining the power of AI with your entrepreneurial spirit. Good luck on your delightful path to AI-driven success!

AI Profit: Harnessing Artificial Intelligence
For Online Wealth Creation

RESOURCES AND FURTHER READING

In this chapter, we provide a comprehensive list of resources and further reading material for those interested in delving deeper into the world of AI and online wealth creation. These resources can serve as valuable references and guides for expanding your knowledge and skills in this rapidly evolving field.

1. Books:
 - "The Hundred-Page Machine Learning Book" by Andriy Burkov: This book is a concise yet comprehensive guide to machine learning, suitable for beginners and experienced practitioners alike. It covers the key concepts and algorithms in machine learning, providing practical examples and code snippets to enhance understanding.
 - "Artificial Intelligence: A Modern Approach" by Stuart Russell and Peter Norvig: Widely regarded as a seminal textbook on AI, this book covers a wide range of topics, including machine learning, natural language processing, and robotics. It presents a comprehensive overview of AI techniques and methodologies.
 - "Prediction Machines: The Simple Economics of Artificial Intelligence" by Ajay Agrawal, Joshua Gans, and Avi Goldfarb: This book explores the economic implications of AI and how it can be leveraged to create value in various industries. It provides insights into the economic principles and

economics-driven applications of AI.

2. Online Courses and Tutorials:

- Coursera (www.coursera.org): Coursera offers a wide range of AI-related courses from top universities and institutions. Some notable courses include "Machine Learning" by Andrew Ng, "Deep Learning Specialization" by deeplearning.ai, and "Natural Language Processing" by University of Michigan. These courses provide an in-depth understanding of AI concepts and practical hands-on experience.

- Udacity (www.udacity.com): Udacity offers nanodegree programs in AI and related fields, providing comprehensive learning paths with a practical approach. The "Artificial Intelligence Nanodegree" and "Machine Learning Engineer Nanodegree" are particularly popular options for individuals looking to enhance their skills in AI development and deployment.

-TensorFlow (www.tensorflow.org): TensorFlow is an open-source platform for machine
learning that offers extensive documentation, tutorials, and examples to help you get started with building AI models. It provides a range of resources for beginners and advanced users alike, including TensorFlow tutorials, the TensorFlow Certifications program, and the TensorFlow Developer Summit conference.

3. Websites and Blogs:

- Towards Data Science (www.towardsdatascience.com): Towards Data Science is a popular platform for data science and AI-related articles, tutorials, and case studies. It covers a wide range of topics, including machine learning, deep learning, computer vision, and natural language processing. The platform features contributions from both industry experts and aspiring data scientists.

- AI Weekly (www.aiweekly.co): AI Weekly is a curated newsletter that delivers the latest news, research papers, and industry trends in AI. It provides a regular update on the latest breakthroughs and developments in the field, ensuring that readers stay up to date with the dynamic landscape of AI.

- Medium (www.medium.com): Medium is an online publishing platform that hosts a vast collection of AI articles and insights. It offers a diverse range of perspectives from experts in the field, covering topics such as cutting-edge research, AI applications in various industries, and ethical considerations surrounding AI development and deployment.

4. Research Papers and Journals:

- arXiv (arxiv.org): arXiv is an open-access repository of scientific papers in various disciplines, including AI and machine learning. It provides access to the latest research papers and preprints, allowing researchers and enthusiasts to stay updated with new discoveries and advancements.

- Journal of Artificial Intelligence Research (www.jair.org): The Journal of Artificial Intelligence Research (JAIR) is a leading publication in the field of AI. It features high-quality research papers and articles contributed by prominent researchers and scholars. Exploring the journal can provide a deeper understanding of cutting-edge AI research.

5. AI Communities and Forums:

- Reddit: The r/MachineLearning and r/ArtificialIntelligence subreddits are active communities where practitioners and enthusiasts share insights, ask questions, and discuss the latest developments in AI. Engaging with these communities can provide valuable networking opportunities and access to a wide range of AI expertise.

- Stack Overflow: Stack Overflow is a popular platform for programming and AI-related questions, where you can find answers to specific technical challenges. It hosts a strong AI community, with experts from diverse backgrounds readily available to help address coding issues and provide guidance. Remember, AI is a rapidly evolving field, so it's important to stay up to date with the latest research, trends, and best practices. Continuously learning and exploring new resources will help you stay ahead in harnessing the power of AI for online wealth creation.

This is just a starting point, and there are many more resources available based on your specific interests and requirements. Remember to adapt and customize your learning journey to suit your individual needs.

Happy learning and best of luck on your AI and online wealth creation endeavors!

BOOKS BY THIS AUTHOR

Naive Publishing: Unleashing The Power Of Words

Discover the world of Naive Publishing, where we believe in the transformative power of words. Our diverse collection of titles is designed to inspire, educate, and entertain readers of all backgrounds and interests.

1. **Journeys of the Soul: A Guide to Transformative Travel** - Embark on a voyage of self-discovery with this all-encompassing guide. Embrace the unexpected, view challenges as opportunities for growth, and create lifelong memories along your journey.

2. **Living With Manic Depression** - A comprehensive guide for individuals and families navigating the complexities of bipolar disorder.

3. **The Serious Side to Humour: Strategies for Addressing Emotive Topics** - Discover how humor can be used as a tool to navigate challenging situations and foster empathy and understanding when addressing personal and societal struggles.

4. **Living in a Postcolonial World: Voices of Marginalised Communities** - Explore the experiences and perspectives of marginalized voices from former colonies, challenging the dominant narratives constructed by colonial powers.

5. **Purrfect Pixels: The Unraveling Love For Cats In The Digital Age And Beyond** - Immerse yourself in the captivating world of

cats and discover the timeless charm, wisdom, and love they bring to our lives.

6. **Unveiling 'The Exorcist': The Battle Of Good And Evil In William Peter Blatty's Masterpiece** - Delve into the chilling world of 'The Exorcist' with this comprehensive analysis of the iconic horror novel and its cultural impact.

7. **Napoleon: A Comprehensive Biography of a Military and Political Genius** - Coming soon!

8. **The Power Of Personal Growth: A Guide To Unlocking Your Potential And Achieving Success** - Coming soon!

9. **Niccolò Machiavelli: The Life and Legacy of a Renaissance Philosopher and Political Theorist** - Coming soon!

10. **Marketing Your Young Adult Graphic Novel: Strategies for Success** - Coming soon!

11. **The Ultimate Cookbook: 150 Recipes, Tips, And Techniques For Mastering The Kitchen** - Coming soon!

12. **Unveiling Panem's Dark Realities: Suzanne Collins' Dystopian Masterpiece** - Coming soon!

13. **Embracing The Magic: A Journey To Pleasure, Freedom, And Love** - Coming soon!

14. **My Nutritional Journey: A Guide to Dieting with Healthy Recipes (The Concise Nutrition and Lifestyle Guide)** - Coming soon!

At Naive Publishing, we are committed to delivering high-quality content that resonates with our readers. Our books are not just about the topics they cover; they are about the journey of self-discovery and personal growth that reading can inspire. Whether you're planning a trip, navigating personal struggles, or simply looking for a captivating read, Naive Publishing has the perfect book for you.

Discover the world of Naive Publishing today and let our books guide you on your path to transformative reading.